Move Over, I'm Driving!
A Road Map for Reclaiming Control of Your Life.

Damian McGee

ISBN: 978-1-7368829-0-0

Library of Congress Control Number: 2021912964

Because of the dynamic nature of the internet, any web addresses or links contained in this book may have changed since publication and may no longer be valid. The views expressed in this work are solely those of the author and do not necessarily reflect the views of the publisher, and the publisher disclaims any responsibility for them.

Published in Los Angeles, California

Printed in the United States of America

To register your book, please visit
www.imdrivingbook.com/bonus

Once you register, you will receive additional bonus
material to accompany the book.

Dedication

To Uncle Mikey

Acknowledgement

To every person I've ever encountered in my life, I say THANK YOU. Some interactions were better than others. Some situations created and left joy, while others created and left pain. Some relationships have ended, some continued, and others are just beginning. Regardless of their current status, they all had meaning and have served a purpose.

To those I knew, those I know, and those I will come to know...Thank You. Every situation in my life teaches me a lesson and ultimately drives me to do and be better.

Table of Contents

Introduction

First, let me thank you for purchasing this book. It is my sincere hope that, no matter your situation, you will finish this book with a new perspective on who controls your destiny.

Because you're reading this, you already may have realized that you don't have the control over your life like you truly desire. You've looked around for answers, and all the "traditional" ideas of moving forward don't seem to work.

Sure, the other solutions sound good - *go to therapy, you have to forgive, you'll find closure, etc.* No matter what you do, the anger, pain, and disappointment seem to linger. You're stuck and unable to level up in your life because these approaches aren't giving you that sense of calm and relief you expected. Well, I'm here to tell you that you still can find incredible levels of success even if you're not quite ready to forgive someone else or if you feel like you're carrying around "baggage" from your previous experiences.

I've been there. I spent years not moving forward because I was waiting to be happy. I was waiting to be healed. I was waiting to forgive everyone. I was waiting for people to forgive me. I was waiting for the closure I was promised. Well, it never happened, and I was miserable.

If you're feeling any or all those things, the good thing is you can stop waiting. Some of those things will resolve themselves over time. You can work on some of those things later, and honestly, some things never will be fixed. However it doesn't matter. You can create momentum, move forward, and create a very successful life just the way you are.

As I coach and mentor people to change their lives, I don't do it from the perspective of life being a singular event that must be done correctly or incorrectly. Instead, my approach focuses on the various situations that alter our reality, cause us to lose focus on our goals, and try to shift our priorities from what we want to what someone else deems to be a priority. I am a "Situation Coach."

Some of the key elements to handling life's situations are having a clearly defined goal or purpose, identifying potential setbacks before they arise, creating a solid plan, and most importantly, identifying the steps you need to take to gain momentum and begin moving forward.

I've spent more than a decade and tens of thousands of dollars researching and analyzing the process of personal development from every angle possible. Three common threads always arise in my research: planning, acting, and momentum. People must know where they want to go, take an initial step to move in that direction, and utilize the momentum they create to move towards their desired goal.

However, most personal development is presented in a way that makes it seem as though everything has to be "okay" for you to become great. Everything must be resolved for you to make a move. You had to resolve the personal struggles in your life to reach greatness. Well, that is not true!

I have not forgiven every person who has wronged me. There are multiple aspects of my life in which I don't have closure. Moreover, many would argue that I still have a few "bags" that I'm dragging along with me. I was also molested as a child. I ran away from home at 16 and was homeless for a considerable amount of time. My first child was born stillborn when I was 19. I dropped out of college. I lost my support system. I've messed up multiple relationships and had many people use and abuse my friendship and love for them.

Despite all of these situations I've encountered, I'm an author and business owner. I've surpassed most of the plans I'd originally set for myself and am working on the next level to those goals. And while I wish many situations in my life had been better and all had reached some point of closure, the truth is they haven't. But the life I desired was not going to wait for everything to "be okay." I'm writing from a place of experience. While I may not have encountered each of your situations specifically, I've dealt with many of the emotions you're facing. Through those emotions, I had to overcome the frustration of feeling stuck while not knowing how to get to the life I desired.

I honestly can't tell you the moment it hit me, but at some point, I realized that happiness and a 'fresh start' hadn't made a date with me. There was no point on my calendar for which things were supposed to get better, and to be honest, I was tired of waiting. I tried to find the joy in a person, in a place, or in a possession, and none of them worked. Nothing external was changing my life. Life kept going, and it wasn't waiting on me to "feel better." HELP WASN'T COMING!

Once I realized that help was not coming, I mapped out

my desired life and constructed a far from perfect plan, and I started making moves. I got in the driver's seat of my own life and took total control and responsibility for my future, and the journey has been amazing. It was not easy, and it was not perfect. I faced internal and external battles that caused me to stop and doubt if I could or should continue, but I did and here we are.

The purpose of this book is to help you reconsider the way in which you've viewed the world around you. I want you to identify things you've let get in your way both consciously and subconsciously. Many times, we've been taught something for so long that we simply act in that manner without questioning its validity or logic. I hope this book helps you begin to question those things.

Question the people and things you have around you and decide whether they are in line with your desired life. Question the social norms of always giving people a pass for the things they do to you despite their relationship to you. Most importantly, question how long you truly want to wait for things to get better before you simply take control and begin to make things happen.

I won't promise you this book will evoke images of unicorns and rainbows. It will challenge some conventional wisdom and possibly even have you struggling with how much you agree with what is being said. Some things in this book directly contradict what you may have been told your entire life. Whatever you do, don't stop. Don't find the sentence you disagree with and put the book down. Push through. When you reach the end, you should be able to take an honest assessment of your situation and determine what things are holding you back. Most importantly, you will understand that you're not waiting for anything to show up. The time to change your life is now, and the person to do it is you. You should not be a passenger in your life, so you need to take control.

You've already taken the first step by picking up this book so let's keep going and watch yourself realize levels of purpose and success that have eluded you for far too long!! A better life is out there. It's simply waiting for you to go live it!

See you on the other side.

Damian

CHAPTER ONE

You Are Where You Are

*If you can't be honest about where you are,
you'll never find a true path to where you
want to go.*

In order to improve our lives stubbornly and unapologetical-
ly, we first must be willing to take an honest assessment of
our current situation. This is not the time for worrying what
others think or taking into account the way we appear to the
outside world. We must start with the willingness first to stop
lying to ourselves, and secondly, we need to update our reality
to match our current situation.

STOP LYING

One of the hardest truths to experience, but also the most
important to accept, was that the most damaging lies in my
life were being told to me by me. Yes, I've told lies to other

1

people, and I'm sure those lies have caused damage. People undoubtedly have lied to me, and those lies caused me great pain. However, the overwhelming lies that delayed my journey and stifled my growth were the ones I continued to reinforce in a manner that didn't allow me to deal with the reality of my current situation.

Tell me if any of these ring a bell:

> » "I'd be in a much better position if I had more time."
> » "If I could get a better job or make a little more money, those problems would be fixed."
> » "I can't do that because there is a system working against me."
> » "I need to get rid of some of this "baggage" before I can make the next move."
> » "People who look like me don't do that."
> » "I'm just waiting for the right time to get started."
> » "If it wasn't for (fill in the blank with any person except yourself), that wouldn't have happened."
> » "I wish I had it like that. They must be lucky."
> » "I'm just too independent for them."
> » "I don't even know how someone could think like that."
> » "I'm just trying to get my ducks in a row (get everything lined up). Then, I'll start."
> » "I don't want to forget where I came from."
> » "They think they are better than everyone," or "I don't want to seem like I'm better than everyone."

» "I don't want to embarrass myself."
» "Of course, it worked for them. They…(fill in the blank with whatever you've made up as the reason for other people's success)."
» "This is all I know, or this is all I've ever seen."
» "I would, but I have to help my (insert relative)."

I hate to be the one to break the news to you, but if you've said any of these statements, the chances are pretty high you were lying to yourself. I know you believed it when you said it. Trust me, so did I. However, as I continued to push forward and analyzed my behaviors, my capabilities, and my perceived limits, I realized that lies like these were holding me back every single day.

Telling these types of lies to myself allowed me not to accept how bad my financial situation was at one point. The lies allowed me to blame others for the countless toxic relationships in which I was involved. Most dangerously, the lies allowed me to limit my own potential due to the circumstances around me. As I'm sure is the case in your life, some of those circumstances may have been outside my control. However, I quickly learned that the manner in which I handled those situations and the extent to which I allowed them to set my limitations was very much within my control.

UPDATE YOUR REALITY

Imagine for a second that you won the lottery. You were just handed a check for one million dollars. The moment you deposit that check, you honestly can state aloud that you are a millionaire. You leave the bank and go buy your dream car for $100,000. You drive off the lot shouting, "I'm a millionaire." You then take your closest friends out to an amazing dinner with great drinks and an open tab. While at dinner, your friends ask you how it feels to be a millionaire, but how can you answer that question when you've only been a millionaire for a few hours? The truth is that you are no longer a millionaire, and at this pace, you soon will be broke.

Yes, you were a millionaire the second you deposited that check into your bank account. However, you stopped being a millionaire the second you purchased your dream car. You will become less of a millionaire with each irresponsible purchase you make thereafter. The problem is not your desire to buy yourself something nice or celebrate with your loved ones. The issue is that your behavior does not support you remaining a millionaire, and that missing step requires you to update your reality constantly. In the case of winning a million dollars, that reality check would be the knowledge of what you have in the bank and what you are willing to spend before you stop making purchases, but we have this same time of behavior in every aspect of our lives.

How many times have you heard someone say that an overweight person who loses weight still sees himself or herself as the chubby kid? How many of us, myself included, go a while without stepping on a scale while we still are squeezing into the clothes we have. How many times have we gone shopping or on vacation and swiped a debit or credit card, but we did not check the balance until we returned only to find out we should have stopped swiping a long time ago? Yes, those examples may seem trivial and may seem like a sign of immaturity in some ways, but we do it in other aspects of our life as well.

Have you ever met someone (or willing to admit this may be you) who claims to be broken and incapable, but that person wakes up and wins on a daily basis? That person may not think he or she is winning, but he or she is overcoming great things and simply doesn't see it. Have you ever seen those who claim to not need or want anyone while they are silently suffering with the isolated approach to life they've created for themselves? Have you seen the people who look you directly in the eye and tell you how happy and confident they are, but when you look through them, their pain and fragility is apparent?

These are all instances of people being incapable or unwilling to update their reality. We want to believe we have it all together, but need to admit we don't. We want to do it on our own, but need to admit we can't. We want to convince ourselves we're incapable of doing something when the reality is we continue to beat the odds at every turn. We just can't or won't update our reality. However, in order to move forward with the greatest chances of success, WE MUST!

TAKEAWAY

None of the guidance you receive in this book (or anywhere else for that matter) will give you the results you want and need if you are unwilling to accept and admit where you truly are.

So many of us live our lives in a way that presents false versions of our reality or sugar coated versions of our problems, and we wonder why the guidance or advice we receive never works. Imagine if you asked someone for directions, but the starting point you gave the person was inaccurate. The directions you received would never get you to your final destination. If by some chance they did get you there, I think we can both agree it will be a much more difficult journey than it had to be if you'd given the person an accurate starting point. If you want **"directions"** to your best self, you first must acknowledge that you are where you are.

1. Now is the time to acknowledge the areas of your life in which you are tired, struggling, confused, scared, and frustrated. There is no need to lie to yourself about it.

2. Many times, our reality, most importantly the potential for growth and change, is much greater than we are willing to accept. Well, it is time to update your reality. If you are reading this book, you still have air

in your lungs, which means you've overcome everything before this moment and still have time to create a future that more closely resembles one of your choosing.

CHAPTER TWO

No Baggage Fees

*Don't worry about a weight limit...grab all
your bags, and let's go.*

Don't stall your progress because you're concerned with the amount of "baggage" you believe you have or have been told you have. Life has no baggage fees. This means there is no cost to you starting before you figure out everything. Some things will figure themselves out. Other things will be key to your development. However, like most vacations, it's hard to know exactly what to bring, so you should bring it all! When you get to your destination (your desired life), you will determine quickly what's needed and what's not.

EVERYONE HAS BAGGAGE

I've always heard the term, "baggage," used to refer to previous decisions, mistakes, pain, and setbacks that somehow are holding us back from greatness as if these moments in our life serve as a sort of ball and chain of despair and limitations. More importantly, we act as though others who have reached certain levels of success either don't have this type of baggage or have somehow rid themselves of every previous setback. What you may be missing is that "getting rid of your baggage" isn't the objective. It's learning how to carry the weight and find ways to use it to your advantage.

If we simply are measuring baggage as the weight of yesterday or the accumulation of mistakes and bad choices we've made, then it's fair to say everyone has some form of "baggage." The problem is many of us have learned that these are the primary markers of our success and our potential. We're reminded of the bad relationships we have experienced and not the many days we endured those relationships or the strength it took to get out of them and rebuild our lives. We're reminded of the bad financial choices we made, but we forget the creative mathematics we learned to pay bills and still provide meals for ourselves and our loved ones. We've learned to romanticize our mistakes subconsciously. We make the negative aspects the heroes of the story. We forget to remind ourselves that we've continued to overcome these moments.

What is even more damaging than our constant obsession with the negative aspects of our stories is the belief that others don't have similar stories. We feel that others who have reached success don't identify with similar struggles and setbacks. Worse yet, we have this idea that these events from our past somehow disqualify us from the greatness we desire. We even spew this destructive language towards one another. "They have a lot of baggage" or "I'm looking to date someone without baggage." Here is a news flash for us all. These people don't exist!! What exists are people who've managed their past and who use it to their advantage or people who've used it to construct a barrier that forever will hold them back.

BAGS OF BRICKS

One of the hardest parts of my personal journey was to embrace the countless moments in my life that were weighing me down. My 'bags' were full of mistakes and bad decisions I made. I had a 'bag' of people I'd hurt and ways in which I'd let people hurt me. I also had a "bag" of stupid financial decisions I made and missed opportunities. My personal favorite bag (I called this one my carry on bag because it never left my side) was filled with every chance or risk I'd taken that blew up in my face. This bag reminded me of every failure, every time I came up short, and just about any other way I could remind myself why I wasn't good enough.

As you may know, these bags can be incredibly heavy. They are invisible to the rest of the world, but they feel as though they are weighing you down like a sack of bricks. Every time something happens, whether you make a mistake, or something is done to you, it feels as if another brick or two is being thrown into the bags. The weight becomes overwhelming, and if we are not careful, it becomes enough to keep us stuck in the same spot forever. We convince ourselves we are not strong enough to carry these bricks of despair and disappointment. We are reminded that no one else is interested in carrying these bricks with us. Therefore, yet again, we feel we are not good enough to do or be better.

You must understand, this situation is not unique to any of us. While our exact situations may not be the same, there is a weight around all of us that challenges us to move forward and take chances. These bricks never stop coming. As long as we are alive, we will make mistakes, be disappointed, and face setbacks. Things will not work the way we'd hoped they would all the time, and some of these situations will feel as though you're adding yet another brick to the bag. However, our job isn't to do away with the bricks.

Our job is not to act as though there will never be negative or painful situations in life. We shouldn't act like people around us won't disappoint us, or we won't disappoint them. Life will still be life, and it is full of unfortunate things that can and will happen to us. However, what we can do is learn how to view these situations. We can change the way we process failures and setbacks. Simply put, we can learn how to repurpose our bricks from being a weight or a barrier to being the foundation upon which we move towards greatness.

YOUR BAGS ARE COMING WITH YOU

At no point will I ever encourage you to ignore or disregard a moment from your life. We may minimize the impact you let it have on your life, but we will never disregard it. Every good and bad situation in your life is a part of you. It is your history. It is your journey. It is your story. The first thing to accept is whether you like it or not and whether other people like it or not, your life is your story. It is a series of events that have led you to this moment.

Notice, what I did not say is that those things are "who you are" because they are not. Part of the problem with how we view our past is we equate situations and setbacks with who we are as a person. You are allowed to have made the mistake of telling a lie, but you are not allowed to be a liar. You are allowed to have been victimized, but you are not allowed to be a victim. You are allowed to have been disappointed or have disappointed someone else, but that doesn't make you a disappointment. We must learn to look in our bags and see all the bricks of our past and understand they are composed of situations and experiences. They are made of choices and decisions, but they are not who we are. They are simply what we have done or had done to us.

Once we make that distinction and learn that we're still capable of defining who and what we are, we begin to understand that we are more than our past. We are more than our mistakes. Yes, we have some form of baggage, and it is tied to us, but it does not define us. Your bags/baggage are just the means by which you carry the experiences of your life.

Therefore, the question then becomes what do we do with those bricks? What do we do with the weight of our past? Some would argue you have to leave it behind. You have to get rid of it to live your best life. This type of thinking is dangerous and unrealistic.

No matter what you do, erasing your past is not an option (minus you losing your memory in an unfortunate accident). We know the things we've done in our lives, and we know the things that have been done to us. In fact, this reminds me of sitting in an airport.

If you've ever been in an airport, there is a constant reminder that you cannot leave your bags unattended. In fact, it goes even further to say that unattended bags will be treated as suspicious items. There is nothing more true in life.

Have you ever met someone who claims to have it all together? This person never has done anything wrong, never made a mistake, and never had a setback. Most of us instantly distrust this person. The person is either lying to us, lying to himself or herself, or both. Either way, we don't believe the person and we treat him or her as suspicious. The person has left his or her baggage unattended, and we don't trust it. We don't trust it because we know that our bags are sitting right there next to us. None of us is perfect, and not one of us is without fault. Therefore, what is the difference between being stuck and finding your roadmap to greatness? It is how you use the bricks inside your bags.

HOW TO USE YOUR BRICKS

Now that we've accepted that the bags are coming with you, we need to decide what to do with the bricks inside them. Most people use the bags in one of three ways: to restrain, to hide, or to succeed. There is not much else you can do with them.

(Actually there is one other way to use your bricks and it may need to be addressed briefly. The worst thing you can do with your bricks is to stand atop them and present yourself as better than others while throwing your bricks of judgement at them. Don't be this person. You may hit a phase where it feels like the only thing to do is defend yourself by hurling these bricks at others, but beyond it being incredibly destructive, it won't bring you joy or advance your position in life.)

Now, for those of us not taking the aggressive brick throwing approach, let's get back to the most common uses of the bricks you've amassed throughout life.

Use #1 - The Restraint

Many of us have convinced ourselves that the moments of the past have proven that we cannot and will not be any better than we are. Nothing in our lives will change including our situation, our environment, or our circumstances. Nothing will get better. We simply are stuck. The weight of our past will ensure that we never make a move forward.

Not only is our baggage tied to us, but also we've placed ourselves in a position that prevents our vision. We can't see a future beyond our past. We've accepted the fact that who and what we are is only inside those bags, and there is nothing more.

Use #2 - The Wall

One of the most common uses of the bricks in our bag is to build a wall around ourselves in an effort to protect us from further damage. We build the wall around our lives, around our hearts, and even around our thoughts. We convince ourselves that the past has proven to us that the way to win is to block everyone else out. We want to safeguard ourselves from pain and negativity. We want to prevent disappointment by not taking chances, and we believe that by making it harder for people to get to us, we will endure less.

There may be a tiny amount of truth to the barrier concept. By referencing your past situations, you can and should use them as a gauge for what you deem acceptable and unacceptable behavior in the future. However, this is very different from simply building a wall and assuming it will prevent the things you hope it will prevent. Most of the time, it actually never prevents future pain or heartache. It prevents growth, new connections, and the type of "get knocked down but get back up" attitude we need to advance in our lives. It is in this space that so many people begin to profess their ill-conceived sense of independence. (We will discuss this more in chapter 6.)

For those of you determined to keep your "wall" up, I give you this idea to ponder. Imagine there is a building with the most precious jewels inside it. Around this building is a wall that seems to be impenetrable. Most law abiding citizens see the wall, and despite their desire to see the jewels, they understand there is no way through the wall. They leave with the desire to learn more and see more of the precious jewels, but they understand there is no reasonable way inside the building. On the other hand, every thief in the area is plotting to get around the wall. They will go over, under, or through the wall if it means they can get to the jewels inside the building, and they aren't concerned with the destruction they may cause in the process.

That precious thing behind the wall is you. It's your heart, your energy, your wisdom, and your personality. It is all the things you're supposed to be sharing with the world. You've chosen to keep those things away from those who may be most deserving and most appreciative of them, but you wonder why those who get close to you still seem determined to do you harm. The wall method has been proven time and time again potentially to block out bad for you, but it equally (and much more effectively) blocks out the good things for you as well.

Use #3 - The Path

Many times, when we consider our ideal state, it feels so far away that it is almost unobtainable. The desire to be better, do better, and have more burns inside us with an unquenchable passion, but the road to this ideal life eludes us at every turn. We feel we don't know enough or don't have enough, or we feel we're simply not worthy enough to have the things we truly desire. Then, to make matters worse, we have this bag of bricks (our past) weighing us down and reminding us of just how stuck we are.

The irony of the situation is that those bricks are your answer! They are the very tools you need to lay the groundwork for the life you desire. So many people suggest we simply must leave the bricks behind as if they were all for nothing. I say that you should use those bricks. Use every single bit of pain you've endured, every tear you've shed, and every disappointment you've overcome. Take each brick and understand what you've learned from the situation that created it. Then, lay it at the bottom of your feet. From there, take another step forward and know you're on sure footing because you're using your previous experiences to guide you.

The bricks become the road you walk to obtain the life you desire. For those of you who have never walked or ridden on a road paved with bricks or stones, I should inform you it is a bumpy road. It is not as smooth as the asphalt and concrete laid for most roads, but it is a beautiful sight to see, and it is a road that gets you there just like any other.

As you begin to lay the bricks of your past down and use them as the path for your future, you first will notice that the weight of those previous situations is becoming a bit lighter. The burden of your previous baggage is beginning to feel much more manageable. Additionally, as you move forward, you can take a look back at any moment and see how far you've come. You can see the many situations and experiences you've had that got you to your current position.

The most effective use of the bricks we carry as part of the baggage of our past is to lay them down one by one and walk on them. Don't just walk on them. Stand proudly on them. Understand that your mistakes brought you here. Your bad decisions brought you here. The pain you endured and the wrongs done to you brought you here. However, you are still standing. You are using those experiences as the bedrock for the life you desire and deserve.

TAKEAWAY

Your past happened, and there is nothing you can do to take it back. Whether it is something you did or something that was done to you, it exists, and the idea that you must ignore it or somehow get rid of it before you can move forward is a lie. You must learn how to use the experiences to your advantage.

Do not let the past restrain you from moving forward. Do not build a wall and block yourself from the many amazing things still available to you. We can't block out pain. We can't put up a barrier against disappointment. Negative emotions and situations are as much a part of the journey as the positive emotions and situations. The goal is simply to accept that those things have happened. Accept each situation for what it was. Understand you can't change it. Instead, you can take each of these experiences and use them to lay a new path that ultimately will guide you to the life you want.

CHAPTER THREE

You Have Enough to Start

*Look in the mirror. This is what we have
to work with, and I promise it is enough
to get started.*

One of the things that we just talked about was accepting your baggage and accepting that things have happened to you in your life. As you're looking at those things or realizing that negative things have happened to you, one of the things that you should not and cannot fall victim to is analyzing everything. In order to move forward, you do not have to categorize your life's experiences as good or bad or right or wrong primarily because those labels are not useful. They are not going to help you. What you need to do is understand that those things have happened.

THE SECRET INGREDIENT IS YOU

One of the easiest ways to waste time when trying to improve your situation is to continue wondering what you need to get started. So many times, we concern ourselves with what we don't have and what we don't know. We forget that we possess the most valuable part of our future life...ourselves! You are the key part of the equation. YOU are the secret ingredient to the recipe that is your success.

Remember, your life is built off of your experiences. You can learn from what others have done and from what others have gone through, but the combination of your life experiences are exactly that...yours! Only you know all the tragedies and triumphs you've faced. Only you know every mistake you've made and every setback you've encountered. You know the totality of your situation, so you are the only one who can lay the path to your desired life.

YOU DON'T HAVE TO DO IT ALONE

Many times when I coach people and one of our first conversations usually includes the phrase "it's on you," they take that phrase to mean they must travel their road alone. This couldn't be further from the truth.

Part of your journey will be identifying the things you don't know and don't understand. The things you know you need to fix or get past, but you lack the information or resources to do it. Don't worry, they will become very clear. The journey to creating the life you want has a very strange way of identifying the things you have all wrong, but that's okay. In fact, that's exactly what we want. As I've heard stated many times, if you want to be better you have to do better. Often, the only way to do better is to learn to do things differently than what you've been taught.

How ironic is it that many of us have insecurities, obvious or hidden, about what we're capable of in this world, but we have the nerve to say "I got it" when someone offers advice or assistance. We are so convinced that asking for information or guidance is a sign of weakness. It is not. In fact, it is one of the greatest signs of strength to be able to look at someone and say, "I can't do this by myself."

If you have trouble admitting the amount of help you need or the number of things you don't know, don't worry, you are not alone. One of the single most difficult things for me to do on my journey was to admit how much I didn't know. I had to admit how much I needed to learn in areas of my life if I truly wanted to do and be better. However, once I admitted my needs, I opened myself up to a wealth of knowledge that was there all along. I learned how to be a better man, better lover, better partner, better father, you name it. I learned how to save smarter, spend smarter, and invest smarter. It didn't matter what it was. Once I admitted to myself how much I didn't know, I instantly felt smarter because I opened myself up to a world of knowledge I avoided, so I didn't look weak or stupid.

DON'T FALL INTO THE TRAP

When you reach this part of your journey, you have to be very careful not to fall into the trap of self-doubt and self-destructive language. I've said all of the following to myself at some point:

"How could you mess that up?"

"Wow, that was stupid."

"What grown man makes that mistake?"

"Why do you keep making the same stupid mistake?"

"Clearly everyone knows but you, so I wouldn't ask."

"You tried, but it's clearly not good enough."

I said so many other incredibly demeaning things just in my own head.

For a while, I spent a lot of time going back over every negative thing in my life. Why did I do this or that? Why did I mess up my relationship or get into a relationship in which the individual did not do right by me? Why did I call these people friends? Whatever you do, do not let yourself fall into the trap of analyzing every bad decision you've made. If you're not careful, it becomes an endless circle of critique and criticism with no actual answers immediately available to you. Sure, there may be reasons, some obvious and some more deeply rooted, for some of these choices, but this is not the time to try to figure out those reasons.

We don't care why that relationship messed up (at this phase of the process). We don't care why you were irresponsible with money. We don't care why you're not where you wanted to be in your career. There will be time to analyze all those things individually, but for right now, we simply need to accept that what happened has happened already. Today is the day you decide that you are going to use everything that has happened to you to start the process to a better life. Some may say, "You should just sit still and "unpack" every negative thing of your past before moving forward." Those same people claim you need to know why things happened to make sure they don't happen again. While I won't say that premise is entirely false, I do believe it is a very slippery slope. The fact is you can't always explain why things happened to you. You can't always explain why people do what they do.

I'm not saying you never will need to find those answers, or a bit of introspective searching is not beneficial. I'm not saying that through growth, you won't discover your own shortcomings and deficiencies. What I'm saying is in order to start moving, you don't have to answer that question yet. I would argue that if you push forward and move towards the life you desire, you quickly will do away with things of the past that did not serve you well. As your desires change, your behaviors will change. As your behaviors change, your habits will change. As your habits change, your beliefs will change. As your beliefs change, your circle might change. This is how you change your life.

TAKEAWAYS

It doesn't matter what you have done in your past or what your current state might be. The version of you that is reading this book is exactly the version needed to start the journey of creating your ideal life. You simply need the following three things:

1. The desire to do better and be better.
2. The willingness to own the process and understand it is your life to create.
3. The humility to admit and accept the things you don't know to allow yourself to grow and learn what you need to learn.

If you can approach this journey with those three things in mind, you are well on your way. Remember, don't fall into the trap of self-critique or criticism as you acknowledge the missteps or mistakes of your past. What's done is done.

*** *Note: The best advice given to me when I used to beat myself up for everything I'd ever done wrong was to remind myself that I'd done the best I could with the information and experience I had at the time. If you can learn to say this to yourself with confidence, I promise it will make self-reflection much easier.*

CHAPTER FOUR

Mother Negative, Cousin Barrier, and Uncle Setback

Family is science, not obligation.

This topic can be one of the hardest for people to accept and address. From day one, we are conditioned to believe our family is all we have. We are told that no one has your back like your family. For some of you, this may be true. For some of you, the group of people scientifically related to you have been supportive, uplifting, and while not perfect, they generally have had your best interest at heart. If that is you, this chapter may not apply to you. For others, the heaviest burden you carry is the weight of your family. It also may be the most important weight for you to set down as you continue on your journey.

THE SCIENCE (WHAT FAMILY IS)

Don't worry, I'm not going to spend the next page boring with you with a high school biology class about DNA and X versus Y chromosomes. However, here are a few quick numbers to consider. You have a 50% DNA match to your parents, an approximate 25% match to your grandparents, uncles, and aunts (not those from marriage of course), and finally a range of 7% - 13% DNA match when it comes to a 1st cousin. These numbers show the extent to which you are connected to a family member by doing nothing more than being born.

This means, if you rip away the sharing of a name and societal traditions that tell you these people must come first, the truth is that you are not connected to anyone on Earth scientifically (unless you have an identical twin) by more than 50% of your being. The important thing to remember is these were people with born-in titles such as mother, father, brother, sister, uncle, aunt, cousin, grandmother, grandfather, on and on and on. You did not pick these people. These people were not selected. These people were not vetted to ensure that they had your best interests in mind. These people are connected to you genetically through science.

THE OBLIGATION

The DNA that connects you to the people who were given assigned titles when you were born will decide your physical features, potential health concerns, and other scientific aspects of your being. Beyond that, much of what makes up you is based on nurture, not nature. The majority of who you are is based on what you were taught (or decided to learn on your own), what you were exposed to (or any actions you took to expand your exposure), and finally, what belief system was instilled in you or that you've cultivated over time through your experiences.

Still, we are constantly taught that if someone is family, they get a 'pass' and should be accepted, forgiven, supported, and defended at all costs. Why is this the case? Does a shared last name make the actions of another individual acceptable? Should a relative be allowed to behave in a way that is less than ideal and should this behavior be ignored for the sake of family?

People are human, and people make mistakes. We're not talking about disowning your son who fails a test or never speaking to your mother who yells at you. We're not talking about the grandparent who thinks this new generation has it all wrong. This is not about seemingly normal occurrences and human error. This is about people who seek to cause you harm or who only can serve as a barrier to your growth. The worst thing is that your family collectively allows the behavior to continue.

One of the hardest truths for many to accept is that sometimes, the people closest to us can and will cause the most damage in our lives: physical damage, emotional damage, mental damage, financial damage, damage to your confidence, damage to your ego, and damage to your courage. These people can be the very barrier on your road to a better you, but you've been conditioned to accept their presence because they are family. These are people who the world says, "Well, you love them unconditionally." However, some of these people will cause you damage that may or may not be repairable as you move on in life.

"YOU KNOW HOW FAMILY IS"

For me, an immediate red flag is when someone says, "You know, family is..." or "You know how your (fill in the blank with a family title) is." These statements are collective excuses that people make for the poor behavior of one or some in the family, and these statements are a subconscious way of telling you that the behavior must be accepted or ignored. THAT IS NOT TRUE! Behaviors considered to be psychologically abusive, physically harmful, criminally inappropriate, and simply against the standards you choose to set for your own life do not have to be ignored or accepted. The idea that these behaviors should be accepted or tolerated is one of the most hypocritical aspects of family dynamics.

Consider the family that tells the young teen girl to look past the inappropriate comments being made by her uncle or cousin because "that's just how they are." Consider the family that tells the up and coming young man or woman that they should stop their journey because they will leave their family behind. What about the family that shuns the individuals who expand their knowledge and experiences to have a more encompassing world view and are told they now think they are better than their family. The worst example is the families who are fully aware of harm being caused by a family member and choose to look the other way. I know firsthand about this experience, and you are not required to accept these types of behaviors just because someone is considered "family."

When I was a child, I was molested by an uncle. He was an

uncle, who according to what we're taught, had the obligation of looking out for my best interests and protecting me as a member of the family. Clearly, that's not what happened. To make matters worse, the rest of my family looked past the behavior despite my revelation, and even my mother continued to be very close with him until his death.

I'm not judging my mother or my family for their decision. The beauty of being an individual is your ability to make whatever decision you believe is best for you. However, remember that this applies to you just as much as it does those people around you. While my family decided that the molestation of at least one family member (potentially more) was not enough to do something about this individual, I decided his behavior (obviously) and their behavior violated the standards I had for the people who would be in my life and the people whom I would call family. These people knowingly and willingly associated with a pedophile, and that was over the line for me. And yes, my feelings against this behavior included my mother.

YES, EVEN MY MOTHER

(I'm only creating this section because people are comfortable with no longer talking to a random cousin or even a sibling at times, but when I make mention of a non-existent relationship with my mother, that seems to evoke a different reaction, so I'm choosing to provide additional insight for you. You are still entitled to your opinion, but I hope you will at least see that I truly believe boundaries and limits for your life are more important than DNA.)

Now, if you're reading this and saying, *I've always been taught to respect my mother*, I assure you so have I. However, respect and obligation are not the same thing. Respect and relationships are not the same thing. Respect and friendships are not the same thing. Respect and forgiveness are not the same thing. Respect and conversations are not the same thing.

There is much about my upbringing and my mother's sacrifice for me I respect and appreciate. This does not require me to sacrifice my limits, boundaries, or self-worth in order to maintain a relationship with her. Now, I know you're wondering, *Why would this guy say I don't have to talk to my mom again?* My story is not yours, and our experiences may not be the same. The boundaries I've set in my life may not be the same as your boundaries, but you should know that no one should be exempt from your boundaries.

I told you I was molested by my uncle. Finally, at the age of 19 years old, I told my mother what happened to me as a child. She had what you would imagine would be the normal reaction of a mother. She was upset. She had moments of blaming herself and wondering what she did wrong. She was trying to figure out why it happened, how it happened, and how she missed the signs. She went through all the things that you would imagine a parent would go through. We had an intense and emotional conversation during which I reassured her that it wasn't her fault. It was something that happened in my life, and it was something that I kept to myself.

After informing the police and being told it was beyond the statute of limitations, we were told that there was nothing left to do but begin the process of healing and move forward with a plan for my life. I knew, even then, I did not want that pain to derail me in any way, and I had to find a way to use the pain as fuel for my forward progress. The problem is the story didn't stop there.

Approximately 12 years later, not only did my mother decide to take my children, my boys, to this same uncle's home for a housewarming party, but I learned that she was still friendly with him. They were having dinner together, and they were hanging out. As I stated earlier, her decision to continue to associate with him was her decision to make, but it was at that moment that I realized I was not obligated to a woman who felt it was acceptable to have dinner with a man who molested me. It was as simple as that. I was not obligated to maintain or sustain a relationship with someone who could break bread with someone who would molest, first of all, any child, but especially her own child.

See, what I did that many of you won't do is I removed the title. Being my mother doesn't give you a pass. Being my father doesn't give you a pass. Being my uncle or my aunt doesn't give you a pass. In fact, if anything, it should make me hold you to a higher standard because, at least scientifically, you should have my back. We're connected. I'm a part of you. Why do we get so mad when strangers betray us when they have no connection to us at all? Why are we constantly providing excuses for people who, at least scientifically, should love us for no other reason than the fact that we're all connected?

I'm not saying it is easy, and I'm not suggesting that you do away with your entire family and go it alone, but I am saying you should pay very close attention to the people around you (even those you are related to) and ensure they are not the ones undermining your progress and causing you the most pain. If they are causing you pain and undermining you, it may be time to create distance and space to allow you to become who and what you want to become.

LOVE FROM A DISTANCE

Many of you are being held back by the same people you're trying to embrace. You choose not to step away from your cousin who is asking for money every single time you see him or her. You choose not to minimize conversations with your parent or grandparent despite his or her constant negativity about every single decision you make. You choose not to separate yourself from the people who don't believe in a better version of you. You, instead, let these people hold you back and drag you down because you share a last name.

When making decisions about the proximity of others to your life, your dreams, and your goals, it is wise to start with your family. In some cases, you may need to cut people off completely, but in most cases, you simply need to create distance between them and you. Occasionally, avoiding that painful Thanksgiving dinner does not mean you don't love your family. It simply might mean you value your peace more than you value their opinions and judgement, or it could mean you're no longer willing to ignore inappropriate behavior or toxic environments.

Whatever you decide is healthy for you, you should know that love isn't based on proximity. You can create distance to maintain sanity, gain clarity, and protect your peace. Your focus should first be on your personal well-being. If you're unwilling or unable to create that distance, you definitely should ensure your boundaries are stated clearly to your loved ones and respected at all times. Don't give away any more free passes because it's easier to overlook bad behavior or negativity than it is to correct the family member creating the negative environment.

TAKEAWAYS

When you are born, you are given a family. There is no screening and selection process. Subsequently, it is imperative you remember a few things:

1. You are scientifically connected to your family members, but this scientific connection does not mean they are entitled to cause you harm, stifle your growth, or undermine your success forever.

2. You are not obligated to accept behavior that goes against the standards you've set for your life just because someone wears a predetermined title (cousin, grandmother, uncle, etc.) and shares less than 25% of your DNA.

3. When people make comments like "You know how family is" or "You know how your aunt can be" what they are saying is we won't or can't do the work to fix this person's behavior, so we will convince you simply to accept it. YOU DON'T HAVE TO ACCEPT IT!

4. Your mother and father are not excluded from these boundaries. They may have much more grace given them because of all they've done for you, but NO ONE should be allowed a free pass to undermine your physical, mental, or emotional well-being.

5. Total expulsion of certain family members may not be
    necessary, but there is absolutely nothing wrong with
    loving from a distance. Proximity does not equal love!

CHAPTER FIVE

There's No Right Time

When I look back on my life, I realize the only
right was right now.

It took me a while to get to this point, but my least favorite time in life is "the right time." The more I experienced and got out of my own way, the more I realized that the right time was simply a stalling tactic, and I was missing every opportunity presented to me to change my life. Those opportunities were being presented to me every second of every day. Those opportunities to change your life are being presented to you every second of every day as well. It's the current moment. It's the present time. It's right now.

"RIGHT TIME" LIST

If I challenged you to list a few goals, dreams, or aspirations you have for yourself, I doubt you would have any difficulty to be able to come up with at least one. Most likely, you would come up with a few examples. If I followed up by asking you what you needed to accomplish those goals, dreams, or aspirations, you'd have the makings of what I call the "right time" list. This would start as a list of things you know you need to do, have to learn, or need to know to start your process. Unfortunately, for many people, that list becomes the very thing holding us back from progress.

Many of us forget the resulting list is nothing more than a to-do list. It's a list of things you can start to do this very second to get moving in the right direction. Instead, the list becomes a sort of ball and chain that you drag along every time you try to make progress. It goes from being a list of things to do to being a list of reasons you can't do something. Instead of being next steps, they become reasons to stall. To make matters worse, we then begin putting delayed timelines on things to ensure we never reach success.

That list becomes the negative talk in your head. It becomes a list of requirements you use to convince yourself you're restricted to inaction because you lack these items. It becomes the reason you can stall and delay. Do any of the following statements sound familiar:

- » "I will start working out Monday."
- » "I will quit smoking after this pack."
- » "I will end this already bad relationship if they do "X" again."
- » "When I get out of debt I will…"
- » "After I read a few more books on the topic, I will…"

The list can go on for many pages, but you are basically saying, "I will do those things I have a strong desire to do when the time is right." There may be things you genuinely can't do because of time constraints or availability, but more often than not, it is a stalling tactic that allows you to continue to feel the comfort of the familiar and allows you to put off the discomfort of the unknown a bit longer.

YOU ALREADY STARTED

It's always interesting to me how clever we are at convincing ourselves that we still are waiting to start something when in reality, we've been on most journeys well before we even realized it. Let's take something as simple as reading this book. At some point, you learned about the book. You sought more information about it, and you eventually purchased a copy of it. You made a plan to read it or set aside time to read it. Now, even if that plan is delayed, and you started reading the book a day or week later than you originally planned to start, the journey to read the book started as soon as you learned about it. To hold the book in your hand and wait for the right time to begin reading is equal to robbing yourself of the work you've done even to get to that point.

Here's another example. Many people want to work out, lose weight, or just create a healthier lifestyle. Just like many of those people, I have had this desire and fell prey to the "starting Monday" or "starting January 1" mindset. We pick a day in the future (delaying discomfort) to 'get ready' (stay comfortable) before we start. However, most of us already know what we need to fix, why we need or want to fix it, what our desired outcome is, what workouts we will do, what changes we'll make in our diet, and what some of the science on our choices shows will be beneficial to us. We even buy food, workout clothes, or workout equipment to get ready. Then, we wait.

You somehow lose sight that you've already started the process. You have momentum, and you stop just short of discomfort and the unknown. We convince ourselves that somehow the circumstance will be better on Monday, January 1, or whatever other random goal post we create to delay our action. Many times, it is simply based on fear. We are not afraid of the thing itself. We are afraid of the discomfort, the hard work, the potential for setbacks, the judgement, and all the other things that come with making significant changes in your life. If you're reading this right now, you've already won countless times and have nothing to fear.

YOU WON LAST TIME

How many times have we heard someone say, "I don't know how I'm going to do this or I don't know how to get through this"? More often than not, they not only survive those situations, but also they thrive because of them. Many times, they survive their challenges with an enviable level of grace and dignity. If you can't recognize it in yourself, reach out to a few of your closest friends, and they may remind you the 'they' who keeps surviving is YOU!

Your bills get paid. You take care of the people and things around you. You've overcome failure, pain, rejection, setbacks, loss, and countless other negative situations. Many times, you weren't even expecting those things to happen, but you survived. Each of those times, you survived with less than you have now. You had less money, less knowledge, less experience, less wisdom, less support, and more. Why would you let something for which you actually have been preparing be delayed?

When you lost a previous job, you managed to make it through, but you refused to apply for a new job while you had one. When you or someone you loved suffered an illness, he or she was forced to change his or her habits, but all you had to do was lay off the sugar and walk every day. You suffered a break up that left you shattered and lost, but you were unwilling to walk away from an unhealthy situation when you could stand on your own two feet because you didn't want to fail or feel lonely.

Time and time again, life delivers blows to us to prove just how resilient we are. Time and time again, we keep winning. The only difference is now you don't have to wait for the world to fall apart for you to make moves. You can start RIGHT NOW! This is the time you were anticipating. This is the time you were hoping would come. This is the day to finish your book and start making changes you know that you need to make. The day to start working out is today. The day to have a salad is today. The day to submit that resume is today. The day to breakup is today. The day to unfriend or block someone is today. You are allowed to be scared of what may come next, but I challenge you to continue reminding yourself of how many times you're already won.

I've gone from being a homeless runaway at 16 years old to making more than six figures not because I made moves at the right time, but simply because I made moves. Plenty of times, people said it wasn't the right time, or it couldn't be done that way, but I did it anyway and here I am. I am better than I was a year ago. A year ago, I was better than five years before that. More importantly, I will be better a year from now than I am today. This is for no other reason than the fact that I decided the time is now to start making moves on the things I desire.

THE PAIN EXISTS NO MATTER WHAT

Did everything work out everytime I took a chance? No. Did everything I've accomplished come without setbacks and struggles? Of course not. However, delaying my start by a day, week, or month wouldn't have changed that. Every action has a reaction. Some are good, and some are bad. Some are easy, and some are hard. Some feel good, and others hurt. Regardless, they are inevitable.

If I work out, I'm going to be tired and sore. If I do it today, I will be sore tomorrow. If I wait three days to start working out, then I'm waiting four days to be sore. I have not changed the end result. I only delayed it. There is not a "right time" to workout that will prevent the soreness that comes from muscle growth and body conditioning. On the other hand, if I start working out today, I will be stronger in a month. If I start saving today, I'll have more money in a year. If I begin removing toxic things and people from my life, I'll have much more peace over time. The changes and 'reactions' I have to things can't be avoided. In fact, many times, putting something off and pushing something back actually makes it harder to start before it makes it easier.

Think about people who want to lose weight, and they say, "You know what, January 1st, I'm going to start to lose weight." They make this decision on December 1st. Some of those people go out, and they buy workout clothes and begin to throw away their cookies. Most of us, and I say "us" because I've been this person as well, look in our pantries and our refrigerators and think, *All right, I've got less than 30 days to eat every bit of sugar in this house.* We overindulge. We send ourselves backwards before moving forward. We are so worried about the discomfort of change that we irresponsibly increase the things that bring us comfort. We act as though that will make it better.

Well, how much more difficult have I made the idea of getting rid of a desire for sugar by consuming it constantly for the next 20 days or 30 days? How much more difficult have I made losing 20 pounds by adding on another three pounds at the last minute? It doesn't make it easier. Did I feel great for those 30 days as I consumed every unhealthy thing in sight? Maybe. However, I did not help my situation. I simply delayed the pain of having to change. In the same way, you delay the pain of going through things, and you delay the gratification of coming out the other side victorious.

TAKEAWAYS

It is said that time is the one thing in life we do not get more of and never can have back. If we can all agree this is true, then it is imperative that you remember:

1. The only right time is right now.
2. Life has demanded you prove how strong you are so use that to your advantage.
3. Many of the journeys you're scared to start you've already been doing the work on. You just need to realize the progress you've made already and keep moving.
4. You've won so many times already.
5. Every action has a reaction, and some reactions are not pleasant, but delaying action doesn't guarantee an increase in positive outcomes. It only delays outcomes.

Chapter Six

You're Not Independent, Nor Should You Want to Be

*I've met plenty of lonely and bitter people, but
I have never met an independent one.*

The idea of stating one's "independence" has become an overused and inaccurate representation of the respective condition of those who scream it the loudest. Nothing in life is done truly independently of other factors. Birth requires participation from a birther. Breathing requires science and plants. Having a glass of water requires systems of filtration and purification. The mere idea that any person exists in this world and is independent of people or processes is absurd.

LITERAL INDEPENDENCE

If we look at the literal definition of "independence" it implies that one is without the authority or control of another.

It reflects how a person is not dependent on another for livelihood or subsistence. If we look at the term through a complete and total literal viewpoint, it would rule out every person in this country. We are all under the authority of control of someone. For most of us, it is our bosses and jobs. It is with every company you sign a contract with for services. It is the people to whom you pay bills, the credit card companies that set the terms of their service, the landlord who sets the terms for their building, and on and on. Every aspect of life is controlled by some version of authority or rule.

For those who think they are not dependent on another for livelihood and subsistence, this is also untrue in the most literal sense. For your livelihood, you need the connectivity of society and the manner in which things are produced and connected. You need a number of people to do their jobs correctly in order to get paid on time. You need a collection of people to do their jobs appropriately in order to go to a store to buy food. Their roles may seem small and mundane, but if you truly understood the process for most actions we enjoy on a daily basis, you might be amazed at the number of people involved in the process.

I know when most people say, "I'm independent," they are trying to state their ability to be responsible for their own well being, to make their own money through existing systems, and to not have their success or failure rest in the hands of another (in a general sense). This is still inaccurate and represents a very limited view of the connectivity of life. I'm sure most, if not all, of us have experienced a time in which we did everything right, but the mistakes of someone else impacted us negatively. Even those of us who have been fortunate enough to start a business are dependent on the consumers of our products and services to be in existence.

The truth is a version of true and literal independence does not exist. For those who successfully are caring for themselves and who do so in a way that has allowed them to limit the outside impact of others actions or shortcomings, I salute you. You are not independent...not in the literal sense.

CONCEPTUAL INDEPENDENCE

If we take a less literal approach, we can look at independence as a concept and simply address the newly understood version of the word which focuses on people having their own opinions, making their own decisions, and financially supporting themselves. If that is the standard by which you choose to stand up and assert that you are 'independent,' then some might agree. The truth is if you are someone who feels the need to profess things like, *Well, I make my own money, and I buy my own things and pay my own bills,* I would still say that's not "independence." That's a mix of maturity and adulthood.

The fact that you, as an adult, have learned to take care of yourself as an adult only makes you an adult. It's called responsibility and accountability. Some people are so hell bent on professing their independence. Why is that?

We opened Chapter 1 discussing why we all need to stop lying to ourselves. This might be a great time to put that into practice. If you or someone you know continuously professes some version of independence, think about when that declaration is most important? When do most people want to make sure you know they're independent? When someone else hurts them? When they feel like they got screwed over? When they feel like they were duped or conned out of something? When they're feeling lonely? When they're confused? When they can't figure out what they're doing or how to get to the next step or how to solve a problem? When they don't want to embrace, acknowledge, or be honest about a mistake they've made or a setback they're having or accept that they need help? In many ways, the term, "independent," has been used to mask pain and shortcomings.

As a child, I remember being told that rich people don't go around talking about being rich. Smart people don't feel the need to prove how smart they are. Equally, those who have become proficient in simply 'adulting' don't need to proclaim it to anyone. In fact, the need to proclaim their independence is hypocritical. If you are truly a person independent of the thoughts, opinions, support, and validation of others, why do you need to prove to those people that you are independent?

Despite the ridiculousness of the claim of independence, I'm aware of its foothold in our social landscape. Being "independent" is a proclamation that I'm sure will be around for a while, especially in circles of people who are NOT living up to their full potential but need to make it seem as though they are. I'm convinced you're reading this book because you want to elevate yourself to a different level, not for the validation of others, but for the pure benefit of yourself and those most important to you. If that's you, let's look at how the world really works and how you will reach new levels of success...interdependence.

INTERDEPENDENCE

Interdependence is exactly what it sounds like it means. It means two or more things that are dependent upon one another. The reasons for interdependence are endless. We can start with the most obvious benefit. Most things are easier when you have someone by your side to assist you. This can be a romantic partner, a friend, a business associate, a mentor, or a coach. Regardless of the person's title, their purpose is to assist you in specific situations to advance your progress and get you to the next level. Reciprocally, they may depend on you for something as well.

Does this mean you can't do anything on your own? Of course not. I'm at a loss when I try to think of something that is done best with no additional support or input from anyone. Just because you can walk alone doesn't mean you should. Whether we like it or not, the truth is none of us are walking a path that hasn't been walked before.

You may think, *Well no one has lived the specific circumstances I have. No one has walked in my shoes.* Well, I never said they had walked the same road wearing the same shoes, but there are thousands of shoes out there, and many of them have walked the same roads you're walking. The question is, do you have the humility to acknowledge that and seek advice and counsel from those people?

If I thought I was the first person to go from zero to six figures, I would be fooling myself. I've walked the road of writing a book, being a sexual abuse survivor, having a poor family support system, learning to manage finances, and constantly learning to be a better man, father, partner, etc. Life is a continuous journey with multiple paths, and I have yet to find one path that has never been walked before.

If you want to be stubborn and defend your need to be 'independent' and ultimately go it alone, that is your right. You are entitled to make your journey as difficult as you deem necessary, but it's unnecessary. Every path is easier with some form of support and interdependency.

WHAT INTERDEPENDENCE LOOKS LIKE

One of the biggest mistakes many people make is trying to control exactly how their level of interdependence looks. They are deciding the type of person from which they will or won't accept help. They are using a false equivalency to convince themselves someone is the right person from which they can obtain information. For example, what if I said I only want to take financial advice from someone who has a nice car. This would be a false equivalency. I have equated their possession of a nice vehicle with the fact that I think they are savvy with managing their money. The person may be good at managing money, but instead of using their car as a gauge to determine this reality, I should want to know what their credit score is, what kinds of investments they have, how they made their money, how they currently utilize their money, and more.

Whatever you do, avoid placing an insignificant requirement on someone that may prevent you from gaining the information you seek simply because of your personal bias. If I said that as a man, I refuse to take advice from a woman, not only would that make me an extremely sexist individual, but also it would have also limited me from some of the most important lessons and information I've gathered throughout my life from some amazing women. For the same reason you may believe that no one has walked in your shoes, you must acknowledge that you've never walked in the shoes of anyone else, and therefore, you have no idea what they can teach you.

Where we mess up a lot of times is trying to find people who have what we have because we don't want to feel like we're losing out. Well, guess what? If they have what you have, you don't need what they have. What good does it do for me to sit across the room from a friend of mine or a stranger, and give him my $100.00 while he gives me his $100.00? We've accomplished absolutely nothing. However, if I have $100.00 and a broken down car, and he's hungry and knows how to get my car running again, now we can swap. "Here's $100.00. Please make my car work." We've now become interdependent and a benefit to one another.

I've gained knowledge from people who look nothing like me. I've exchanged resources and ideas with people from very different upbringings and backgrounds than mine. I still gain knowledge from friends and associates who live in different places, have different lifestyles, and are reaching for different goals. The differences are what make us unique and able to sustain our own livelihoods, but it is our interdependency that makes us better.

Every aspect of your life should have some version of interdependency if for no other reason than a periodic sanity check. The longer you try to ignore that, the harder you're making your journey.

THEY ARE NOT ALL BAD

Many times, when I discuss this level of interdependence with people, they like to remind me of every time they've been hurt or "screwed over" because someone has let them down. I genuinely understand their perspectives. I told you my own mother was having dinner with my molester. I don't know how much greater disappointment there can be, but that doesn't change the fact that I still need to be connected to people in order to be successful.

Not everyone is out to get you. I do not doubt you have encountered people who seek to use or misuse your time and attention. In fact, I do not doubt you will encounter more of those people. However, shutting out the endless knowledge and support available to you because you've encountered a few 'bad actors' is only increasing the damage those people have done. If someone already has hurt you or taken advantage of you, don't let them have that control endlessly by keeping well-meaning people from your circle.

If you find yourself constantly being taken advantage of or let down, I would argue the problem is one of three things: 1) You very much need to change or expand your existing circle of influence; 2) You have not set hard enough limits and boundaries that ensure when lines are crossed, people are removed from their existing place of trust or responsibility in your life; and/ or 3) You have set unrealistic expectations for the person and blurred the lines of his or her purpose and significance. Simply put, imagine having a friend who is always broke, but loves to spend your money, so you decide to let them be your accountant. Then, you say later, "I don't trust people's financial advice because the person who helped me before screwed me over."

I'm sure you caught the ridiculousness of that concept, but we do it all the time. You will meet bad actors. Nothing I say can prevent this, but I can assure you the more you open yourself up to the possibility of interdependency, the more you will find the right type of people. The best part is when you get around people who are not trying to hustle, it's easier to identify people who are trying to hustle. When you surround yourself with people who actually are getting results and moving forward in their lives, it's easier to identify people who are just talking but actually are not doing anything.

Additionally, the more you surround yourself with people who are doing things the right way, it helps you self-reflect. If I may, let me let you in on a little secret. When you are around a person or people who regularly make you say, "I never thought of it that way" or "Wow, I've been looking at this all wrong," then you are usually on the right track.

We are all surviving, so I'm not here to judge and say you are wrong in the things you do and the way you do them. In fact, if you are taking care of yourself and continuing to push through, then I would say you are doing everything right. However, trust me when I say there are people who's 'right way of doing things' looks nothing like your way. Their way is much easier, and it generates far greater results. Find those people!

TAKEAWAYS

While the idea of being 'independent' has become ingrained in society, the truth is a literal sense of independence doesn't exist, and a conceptual version is a misrepresentation or mask to true feelings. This doesn't stop people from constantly proclaiming their independence. However, if you want to move to the next level of your life, the truth is:

1. Being an adult is simply being an adult.
2. Those who proclaim their independence the loudest are usually masking other pain or emotions.
3. Going it alone is possible but not recommended.
4. Interdependence is the key to continued growth and an increased level of awareness and access to new information.
5. If everyone you encounter has done you wrong, you should change your circle or set much stricter boundaries.

No concept is foolproof, and being interdependent does open the door to people who do not have your best interest at heart. However, increasing the number of truly positive and well-meaning people around you will help you more readily identify those who should be cut from your circle or at least moved to the outer circle of the life you're trying to create.

CHAPTER SEVEN

Gaining Some Closure on Forgiveness

Closure is a lie and forgiveness is unnecessary.

I'm going to say what many people won't say and what many others need to hear. Closure does not exist in the simplistic form in which we speak about it, and forgiveness isn't as necessary as everyone would have you believe it is! I know most religions teach that forgiveness is critical to reaching some greater version of yourself. Since many of us were children, we were taught you must forgive to be healed. Well, I'm not here to argue those teachings directly. However, I am here to talk to the people who have lived long enough to know that 'closure' never really feels closed, and I want to talk to those who see some situations and simply say, "I have no interest in forgiving that person."

CLOSURE

Tell me if any of these statements sound familiar to you:

» "I just need closure."

» "We are seeking closure."

» "I hope that provides some closure."

» "I'm sure they can move on once they have some closure."

The term 'closure' is one we hear used often when it pertains to pain and tragedy. Breakups, deaths, crimes, and things that leave us seeking answers and clarity all somehow revert back to a desire for closure. In fact, many times, the term is used in a way that signifies that once we reach a specific point in life, closure is guaranteed. The truth is, it is not!

In fact, most things we experience in life involving significant loss, trauma, or emotional pain rarely have the desired 'closure' associated with them. For some of these situations, we find the answers we seek, but for many situations, we don't get that closure. We slowly come to a point of acceptance and hopefully resilience, but I would argue closure is a misrepresentation of what we are experiencing.

If you've ever been a victim of a crime or lost someone due to a senseless act of violence, there is no closure to that. You hopefully get answers or justice, but is that truly closure? When your spouse of 10 years mysteriously finds a new partner and walks away with no explanation (or a bad one), is there closure on that type of confusion and loss? There is acceptance, and I hope resilience, but for most people, there is always a piece of that pain that will linger. We compartmentalize feelings. We find coping skills, and we move on, but many times, these things aren't completely closed.

My Uncle Michael (obviously not the one who molested me) still sits in my top 5 list of the greatest people to have ever lived. Most of us have at least one person like this in our lives. The person is irreplaceable, and his or her wisdom and advice rings true in the most random situations and during the most trying times. The person's presence in your life was integral in molding the person you are today. For me, that was Uncle Mikey (as we called him).

Uncle Mikey died from cancer at the incredibly young age of 43. He died in his own bed. He was a shell of himself. The man who once was the life of the party and would hand you his plate of food and ignore the rumble in his own stomach took his last breath. I was 19 years old, and I was absolutely devastated. That day, which I can still recall vividly, tore me to pieces. After more than 20 years, there is no closure. There is acceptance, and there is damn sure resilience, but there is no closure.

I don't feel sad or cry on a regular basis, but I can tell you wholeheartedly there are days I wish I could just have one more day to show him what I've accomplished. I want to introduce him to my family. I want to prove I was listening to his advice. I'm fully aware I'll never have that day, but for a split second, those thoughts resurface a pain reminiscent of the day I lost him.

I'm not the only person who has experienced this type of loss. Some have lost a parent, child, or other loved one. Some have lost a significant relationship or simply had their livelihood yanked from them in an instant. For many people, that type of loss and pain is never "closed". It calms down over time. It becomes more manageable or bearable. We stop asking why as often and begin to accept what simply is, but the story is never closed.

USE THE PAIN

If you've connected with the idea that some painful things in your life are never closed, then it is important to understand that I'm not making this point to justify those who sit in misery and use it as a barrier or deterrent to reaching new levels. In fact, I bring it up so you will do the exact opposite. I want you to understand that it's okay if you're still hurting, and you're still looking for answers. It is okay if you don't obtain that "closure" everyone says you should have. What is not okay is to let that stop you from still making positive moves in your life.

Think about the closest person to you and think about something unfortunate happening to them. There's nothing that I can say to you that would close that wound. There's no amount of justice, sorrow, or condolences that makes that pain go away. Time, understanding, support, and acceptance make it bearable, but it's never 'closed.'

Whatever the situation may be that caused the pain, you have to decide how to move forward with it. Will you let it control your emotions forever or cause you to see everyone you encounter negatively because of a previous situation? Will you let it paralyze you from believing you deserve or are capable of more because the previous situation included something you believe to be a failure on your part? Will you find a way to use that pain as the fuel you need to drive you forward? It doesn't mean you won't still hurt, but sometimes, just wanting and needing something "better than this" might be all the reason you need to keep going.

Having "closure" is not a requirement for progress. Unfortunately, some of the most critical times in life will require movement through pain, fear, and grief. There is a reason people say things like, "We have to get up and keep moving" when life knocks us down. I experienced it myself. When my Uncle Mikey died, I didn't know what to do with the pain I felt, but I made a decision to channel all that energy into creating a man who would make him proud. I am not a perfect man, but I am one who could survive and didn't just roll over because life got hard or because I made some mistakes.

The same is true for you. Whether you lost someone special or are experiencing pain from other challenges in life, the goal still should be to repurpose that pain and use it as fuel (motivation). My fuel was a life never lived by my uncle, and 20 years later there's still no closure on the pain I feel for his loss. However, the fuel is continuous, and therefore, my progress is continuous.

GIVING FORGIVENESS

If you grew up around a church like I did, you probably remember the countless times you were taught or told about forgiveness. You were reminded constantly that you had to forgive others. You may have been told the lie that you never would move forward and find happiness until you forgave those who wronged you. Guess what? Yes, you can. In fact, not only can you move forward without forgiving people, but also many times, those you want to forgive can't be forgiven until you make moves in your life to find the necessary space and mindset to forgive them, if you choose to forgive them.

I told you about my mother and the pain I experienced when I realized she was spending time with my uncle who molested me. Somebody asked me if I forgave her for that now that he's dead. Honestly, I don't think so. I don't know that a day could ever come when I could understand such a betrayal, especially now that I'm a father and understand that bond. Contrary to what many might have you believe, that lack of forgiveness is a non-factor in my life.

Not feeling the need to forgive someone who has wronged me to that extent doesn't change the circumstances of my life. It doesn't change the drive I have or the need I have to create the best life for my family. It doesn't change my ability to love others and enjoy the love bestowed upon me. I made a choice to accept that she made a choice, and we all live with them. While you may believe forgiveness is ideal, it is not required.

THE MISCONCEPTION

The idea of forgiveness gives people a false sense of 'closure,' and we've discussed that term in detail. The idea that forgiving someone somehow will make you feel better is not guaranteed. I completely understand the concept and why people say it. I simply think it's B.S. People make choices about how they want to treat us and the things they believe are acceptable to do to us. If those things cause you significant pain or harm, the only two people asking you to forgive that person are the person who committed the act and someone who isn't feeling your pain. Neither of them are qualified to tell you what is and isn't acceptable for you.

When people make choices about how they treat you they make the choice to deal with consequences of that choice. The important thing to note is that not forgiving is not the same as never letting go. You don't need to wallow in the grief or constantly remind the perpetrator of the offense. You don't need to change who you are and become bitter or jaded. You simply need to acknowledge its existence and decide a healthy way to cope with the consequences.

For example, let's say you are in a relationship, and your partner cheats on you. The things you're most likely to hear are:

- » "Can you or did you forgive them?"
- » "How did you forgive them?"
- » "I can't believe you forgave them."
- » You will ask your friends, "Should I forgive him or her?"
- » You may say, "I don't think I can forgive him or her."

If I were the friend you called at that moment, my starting point would not be a conversation of forgiveness. I would ask quite simply, "Do you believe this is something you can overcome and stay in a relationship and how does it mesh with the boundaries you set for yourself and your life?" To me, these are the questions that should be answered before any form of forgiveness is even discussed.

If you choose to leave the person, the idea that you did or didn't forgive them becomes trivial. It has no significance except to give other people a method by which they can claim you've moved on. You know another way of showing people you've moved on? Grab your things, move out, take time to process the pain, find a new partner who respects you and your boundaries, and find true joy and peace. Did you see forgiveness in that process? You didn't because it's not necessary. Boundaries, limits, space, time, and progress are required, but forgiveness is not required.

GETTING FORGIVENESS

Understand that forgiveness is not something that you are required to give. Additionally, it is not required for you to receive forgiveness from others. I'm not perfect, and I'm guilty of making countless mistakes in my life. Some of those mistakes have caused pain for myself, and other mistakes have caused pain for those around me. People say that we must seek forgiveness, but this perspective makes the assumption that everyone is sorry, and others are seeking to forgive you.

Most people don't like to discuss this fact, but the truth is sometimes we do things that may not be ideal for someone else, but they are necessary for our own sanity, safety, or peace. For those things, we should not be sorry, even when these things cause others to have hurt feelings. This does not mean we should justify being malicious or mean, but it does mean that every action we take won't make sense to everyone, and that is not a reason to seek forgiveness.

On the contrary, there are things we do that absolutely inflict pain on others, and those things are well outside of what should be acceptable behavior. Sometimes, we know as soon as we commit the act, and other times, we learn about our mistakes as we grow and experience more of life. Regardless of the intent, we must be honest with ourselves and understand that others are not obligated to give us the forgiveness we seek.

I firmly believe we are not obligated to afford everyone the forgiveness they seek, but this also means others are not obligated to forgive us. This is important because many people stand still while they are waiting for forgiveness. They cannot move on to new things unless an action or a situation is forgiven. This is dangerous because you leave your ability to move on in the hands of others. While I encourage you to seek forgiveness if you are truly sorry for your actions, please don't let the need for forgiveness stop you from moving forward.

While we can find the ability to move past our mistakes, others may not be able to move forward, and that is okay. Moving forward does not mean you are disregarding their feelings or the pain you may have caused. Instead, moving forward represents accepting it and allowing people to give you the grace they decide to give when they decide to give it.

(Side Note: The truth is I hate the phrase, "I'm sorry." Don't talk about how you'll do better, DO BETTER! Don't talk about when you'll be better, BE BETTER! A true apology comes in the form of changed actions.

Sometimes, you can demonstrate that you are going to do better in front of the person whom you harmed and in a manner that allows the person to experience your changed behavior. Other times, you move on from that individual to allow him or her the time and space to heal from your mistake and give yourself the time and space to grow into a better person.

When you discover you've done wrong, the easiest way to show you're truly apologetic is to DO RIGHT!)

ANTI-FORGIVENESS

When I speak to people about this topic, they believe I am against the concept of forgiveness in its entirety. That is not at all what I'm saying. If you strongly believe in forgiveness or the need to forgive others, then you should do that. My point is not to say that forgiveness is a bad thing. My point is that many times, the idea of forgiveness causes people to lie to themselves about the extent to which they've accepted or dealt with an issue.

How many times have you or someone you know said they've forgiven someone, but they bring up that issue every chance they get. How many times have you heard someone say, "I forgive them, but it still hurts." This is because the concept of forgiveness isn't solving anything. The majority of people I've seen who "forgive" are just holding on and continuously punishing people for their actions. That person is just uttering the word forgiveness because somebody told him or her it was the right thing to do.

This primarily happens because people are told that forgiveness is not for the other person. It is for them. Well, what is it doing for you? Do you hurt less because you forgave them? Did it erase the incident from your memory and undo the broken trust or embarrassment? Of course, it did not. We've been so programmed that forgiveness is essential that we wouldn't dare question its necessity. However, if you consider your experiences and your past, I would argue the people who have most requested (sometimes even demanded) forgiveness are those who've done the most unforgivable things.

The fact is you don't owe anyone forgiveness. You can choose to give it. I'm not opposed to anyone forgiving someone else if they need to do so. However, you also can choose to move on without forgiving someone else and simply make the incident an experience from which you learned a valuable lesson, and the person becomes a thing of the past. Whether or not you forgive the other person is your choice. I'm simply saying don't fall victim to this concept that you have to forgive everyone for everything.

You may encounter people who are deserving of your forgiveness. These people are sorry for things that they do to you or for the pain they may have caused you, and their mistakes were within your limits of forgivable things. On the other hand, there are people who are not deserving of your forgiveness. They could care less about the impact they've had on you. You are not required to forgive those people!

TAKEAWAYS

1. Not every situation has a point of closure. Knowing this can save you a lot of time and energy and prevent you from looking for something that doesn't exist.

2. When the pain doesn't subside easily, repurpose it and use it to fuel your momentum and forward progress.

3. Stop letting people tell you that everything and everyone must be forgiven. Everything is not forgivable, and everyone doesn't deserve your forgiveness.

4. Despite what others may tell you, growth and success are possible without forgiving every person who has wronged you.

5. You are entitled to forgive if you choose to do that, but don't lie to yourself just to say the words. The honesty of saying "You don't deserve my forgiveness" is far more rewarding than the lie of undeserved or insincere forgiveness.

Chapter Eight

Your Reality Is Not The Only Reality: Two Things Can Be True

Everyone is right, and everyone is wrong.

When thinking about the journey of personal development and growth in my own life, I believe the most
enlightening moment for me was a true understanding and
appreciation that my right did not equate to another person's
wrong. It wasn't my job to compare my reality to someone
else's reality. Instead, it was my responsibility first to understand and appreciate my reality and then begin taking the steps
to change the things I didn't like. Too many people waste time
trying to change the reality of those around them while they
are not embracing or altering their own reality. The more you
can live your life with the approach that those two things can
be true, the more receptive you will be to the idea of growth
and new realities.

FOR YOU TODAY

When reality is defined, it refers to the state of things as they actually exist, whether it's the world around you, your home life, your family situation, or just your perception of the world. Those things constitute your reality. However, when I think of that definition, I feel as though they should have added three words - "for you today."

With this shift, reality would then loosely be defined as the state of things as they actually exist for you today. The reason I believe the addition of those three words is so significant is because it gives you the option to alter your reality at any time. The idea that you could look at your life and understand that while this (whatever 'this' means to you) is your reality today, you have the ability to alter that reality at any moment would be incredibly freeing. Your reality may have you bogged down with incredible debt, a job you hate, trouble in a relationship, or any of the many other things many of us experience. However, the second you decide that while that is your reality today, it doesn't have to be your reality tomorrow, things immediately begin to shift.

Have you ever heard someone say things like, "Well, this is the life I was given" or "That may be your reality, but it's not mine"? It pains me to hear people use such a finite description of their situation because they've decided there is no alternate reality for them. They've decided the cards they were dealt are the only cards they get to play. What they don't understand is that while life dealt you a handful of playing cards, the game of life is a game of Gin Rummy - a game in which you actually control your cards.

A GIN RUMMY LIFE

As I was writing this, I had to embrace my age and understand that some of you may not know what Gin Rummy is or have never played the game so let me provide a bit of context. I won't bore you with the entire rulebook of the game, but the concept is important. In the game of Gin Rummy, each player is dealt a set of playing cards. Some of those cards will be the same suit (spade, diamond, heart, or club) while others will be of the same face value (Ace, Jack, 9, etc.), but the key is you have no control over what cards you are dealt. The existing cards are the reality of your life.

Now, in order to play the game, players take turns pulling cards from the pile of cards in the center. If they want to keep the card because it will help them build a set (three of the same value or three sequential cards of the same suit), they get rid of a different card. If they don't want to keep the card, they simply throw it down and wait for their next turn. As the game progresses, the option is to improve your hand until all of your cards are in a set (or 'run' officially). Once this happens, you lay them down and are awarded points.

While I love the game of Gin Rummy, it is not important to me that you ever play it. However, it is such a simplistic version of how you can and should approach your life. You absolutely should understand the concept. In the game of Gin Rummy (and life), if you simply take the cards dealt to you and sit back as others go around swapping out their cards, you are guaranteed to lose. However, if you look at your hand and understand that what you were dealt is only to start the game, you quickly will realize there are many rounds in which you will have the opportunity to change the cards in your hand. Change your reality. Change your life!

The hand you're dealt (left) doesn't have to be the hand you finish with (right).

REAL, ROMANTIC, OR RIDICULOUS

As we discussed previously, lying to yourself doesn't allow you to assess your current situation accurately. When you don't truly embrace the world around you as it exists today, you increase your chances of making the wrong decisions about how to move forward. It is imperative that we start from an honest understanding of our current reality. The problem is that many of us have either a romantic or a ridiculous version of reality.

The most common reality is unfortunately the ridiculous version. This is simply the idea that there is no other option. Too many of us confuse the idea of reality with finality. Nothing in life is final until it ends. You don't believe me? Ask the person who starts a company after a messy divorce at the age of

50. Ask the person who suffers a tragic injury and is told he or she never will walk again, but subsequently he or she runs his or her first marathon. Finality only comes when we convince ourselves there is no other option and refuse to move.

I don't call it ridiculous to offend anyone who may be experiencing the mindset. I promise you I had many times in my life when I nearly fell victim to it. I call it ridiculous because a different reality is usually so incredibly close. As they said when I was growing up, "If it was a snake, it would have bit you." I can't tell you how many times I've spoken to people who 'ridiculously' have accepted that their current state is their only state, but we discover that an alternate reality is an email, a phone call, a break up, an interview, a budget, a book, or a training session away.

Let's not downplay how we start to believe there are no other options. Significant loss, lack of information, extreme betrayals of trust, and so many other things can convince us that 'this' is all we're ever going to be or get. I understand that exhaustion or defeat can make us feel as though the current reality is the only reality. Despite loss, failure, or a simple lack of knowledge, the ability to refocus and change one's reality is much closer than we sometimes allow ourselves to believe. It's not ridiculous to feel the things you feel or struggle with the things that plague you. It is, however, ridiculous to believe that your reality today is the only reality available to you because that is not the case.

The other potentially dangerous version of a person's perception of reality is the romantic version. These are the people who spend countless hours convincing the world (and themselves) their reality is different from what it is. It's the person who is so disillusioned with the need for external approval that they refuse to embrace their current situation in an effort to move themselves forward.

For example, imagine a person who doesn't have a car and walks to a public bus stop to get to work every day. (P.S. I am not shaming public transportation because it was my only transportation from ages 14 - 20.) This person knows he or she needs a car and has managed to begin saving a tiny bit of money to purchase one. However, instead of acknowledging this, he or she stops by a specific car on the way to the bus stop and takes a picture standing by it to post on social media to give the impression that he or she owns the car. Despite not having a vehicle, he or she is romanticizing the reality to convince others his or her world looks different than it actually does.

Some of you might be saying, there was no harm and no foul. For the most part you are correct, but ask yourself this, "How does this picture help this individual?" He or she may feel better momentarily and may enjoy the comments that come from the social media world. When all is said and done, he or she has done nothing to help his or her current situation. What if this same person posted the following message?

"Tired of riding the bus everyday. Saved $2,500 for a car. Does anyone know someone with a cheap car to sell or who is willing to help me get in one. I can work for it and pay it off."

This type of post requires a different level of humility or honesty, but it allows people to help this individual because they know his or her actual situation. When we pass the picture of the person standing by the car he or she doesn't own, we continue to scroll and think nothing of it. By romanticizing his or her reality, this person is not allowing the opportunity for growth or assistance.

I know this is a simple example, but so many of you are standing by cars and houses you don't own. You are standing by men and women you don't love (or worse who don't love you), or you are smiling endlessly at jobs you hate. Stop romanticizing a reality you don't enjoy and begin to change it.

YOURS IS NOT THE ONLY ONE

We've discussed that an alternate version of reality is available for you should you desire it, but I believe it is also important to acknowledge that your reality is not the same as other people's reality. One of my favorite sayings amongst my friends and me is that two things can be true. When we only can see the world and others through our reality and do not take the time to consider their reality, we miss an opportunity for growth. We miss an opportunity to expand our knowledge and awareness of the world around us.

What if I told you going to college was the best decision I ever made because it prepared me for the career I have today? It would be a true statement if it was my reality. What if I said going to college was the worst decision I ever made because it left me with $250,000 debt. This could also be true if it was my reality. The problem is most of us don't take the time to understand why someone is saying something or how their reality might be different. We simply impose our circumstances, perception, and belief system on them.

In the college scenario, most people only hear "College was the worst decision" or "College was the best decision," and they begin to approve or disapprove of the sentiment based on their personal experiences. The fact of the matter is for two different people, those things both can be true. To be honest, both statements could be true for the same person! We must understand that another person's reality is not our reality, and therefore, our job is not to agree or disagree with someone else's reality. Our job is to seek to understand it and find ways to learn from it when possible.

One person might make $50,000 a year and barely pay all his or her bills. Another person may make the same amount of money, but the person may vacation with his or her family twice a year. Most people waste their time debating the value of $50,000 as if there is only one reality for that amount of money. What's more beneficial and what I challenge you to do with every situation you encounter is to seek to understand how each person uses that equal amount of money. Learn the tricks of the vacationer and the mistakes of the person who is struggling and adjust your own life accordingly.

Everyone's life and circumstances are different. Everyone's life is an ever-changing result of continuous choices. In many ways, this makes us a group of walking experiments of what to do and what not to do in order to live a better, more productive life. Don't waste your time arguing about right or wrong. For one person, college was the best decision, and for the other person, college was the worst decision. In the eyes of one another, both people are right, and both people are wrong.

When we learn to live a life that honestly embraces our current reality and the ability to change that reality while also acknowledging that another's reality may be different, and their reality doesn't have to impact our own reality, we begin to live a life free from the burden of always being right or wrong. Instead, we live a life focused on simply being better.

TAKEAWAYS

1. Your reality is what is true for you today, but is not limited to what is true today.

2. Don't romanticize your reality to the point that you lie to yourself and others instead of embracing the truth.

3. Don't be 'ridiculous' and convince yourself there is no better option than your current reality.

4. The cards you were dealt are not the only cards available to you. You don't like the cards you're holding? Pick up a good one and discard the bad ones until you get the hand you want.

5. Two things can be true. Your job is not to be right or wrong. Your job is to be better.

CHAPTER NINE

Your Future is Paved by Your Past

*Bricks are heavy to carry but make
a great walkway.*

In Chapter 2, we discussed the baggage we all carry and the manner in which these various life experiences can become a restraint, a barrier, or a walkway. In that chapter, I presented it as if it were an option, but if you've made it this far in the book, you clearly seek to grow. Now would be a perfect time to inform you that it's not an option. If you want to grow and build the life you want, those "bricks" you carry around will be laid down as the very foundation on which you will walk to achieve your ideal life.

BRICK ROADS HAVE BUMPS

When I first explained my "bricks as the path" theory to a friend of mine, he suggested I find a way to change the image to concrete. He suggested I turn baggage into bags of concrete, so when it came time to lay the path, the road would be paved with concrete. In his mind, he wanted the illusion to be that we could create a journey that was smooth and even if we did the right things and learned from our mistakes. In his mind, it would look better to show a path without a rough surface or additional friction. He was wrong!

The truth is your journey will not be smooth. The path you lay will not be perfect, and it will not be without errors. That's okay. We are not seeking perfection. We are seeking movement. When you move, you may trip and fall. You may even get hurt, but keep moving.

No matter how much I learn or experience, I have yet to find a system for growth and development that can guarantee a smooth road ahead. In fact, if you are considering a program or a mentor who tells you everything will be rainbows and unicorns, you should save your money and run away as quickly as possible. Remember, we are seeking improvement not invincibility. A road paved with the 'bricks' of your past will be a bit uneven. It will have surfaces that are incredibly smooth and others that are a bit rougher. Some will fit together perfectly, while others need a bit more force to put them in place. Most importantly, everyone else will have an opinion on which way you should construct your path, but the journey is yours and yours alone.

If you have a chance you should look up a picture of the Red Brick Roads in Pullman, Washington or the Original Route 66 Brick Road, what you may find is that these roads are not put together perfectly. You will see all the bricks are not the same color, and some are more worn than others. In fact, I'm sure if you visited either location, you would see the countless flaws within each brick and the unevenness of the road. However, if you take a step back and look at the road in its entirety, there is a certain beauty to it. It's not fancy, but it's effective. It's not shiny, but it's stable. It may not be smooth, but it will get you where you want to go.

Your journey will be the same. Don't worry about the lack of perfection as you create your path. Don't fear the bumps you have or will encounter. Don't ignore the older lessons that may be a bit more worn but still can play an integral role in creating your path. Your past is yours. Your wins and losses are yours. Your successes and mistakes are yours. Your bricks are your bricks. Use them all as the foundation needed for you to move forward.

MOMENTUM IS KEY

Starting any process or journey can be difficult. So many people act as though their experiences are being tossed into a bag or a box, and with enough bad experiences (bricks) being put in there, the bag soon will become too heavy to carry. If you believe that, you are correct, but if you look at the illustra-

tion of you carrying "baggage," you will see there are wheels. Life is designed for us to keep moving, so those wheels become very important.

If you can agree not to accept the 'ridiculous reality' that your past forever will weigh you down and prevent you from moving forward, you will see there are ways to make progress even with your "baggage." Use the wheels available to you and continue moving forward. While I don't want to insult your intelligence as if you don't know this, I want to shout from the rooftops that once you start moving them, wheels become so much easier to move.

Your journey will be the same. When you start making hard decisions, taking difficult steps, having those hard conversations, or embracing some harsh realities, you will begin the initial pull on your past and begin creating momentum. I won't bore you with a physics lesson on force and momentum, but I think it is important to note the most energy you will have to exert in this process is the initial pull to get the wheels moving. In life, it could be the initial decision that enough is enough and the reality you have is not the reality you want, and you're ready to do something about it.

Once you refuse to settle and act on the desire for more, those wheels will begin to turn. The wheelbarrow hooked to you will begin to move with you as you start your journey towards something better. Forgive me for sounding like a TV infomercial, but that's not even the best part.

When you begin to use your past as lessons, motivation, and fuel, you will begin to lay those bricks down as we discussed. At the same time you will be reducing the weight of your wheelbarrow. (BTW, if the wheelbarrow thing is bothering you, I'm originally from parts of the United States where you know what a wheelbarrow is. Feel free to replace it with a utility wagon, a quad fold cart, a dolly, or whatever. Who cares, just get moving!) When you put yourself in a position to create momentum by moving forward while reducing the weight of previous decisions and experiences, you will be amazed at your ability to keep going. Your speed will increase while the resistance decreases. This is, by definition, momentum.

TAKEAWAYS

I will never try to encourage or teach someone to ignore or disregard their past. The lessons we learn with every circumstance we encounter are much too valuable to disregard them. Instead of ignoring the things we've experienced and encountered, we must understand that in order to move forward:

1. Every experience you've had can and will help you lay the foundation for a road to move forward.
2. That road is not guaranteed to be smooth or perfect.
3. Life was designed for us to keep moving.
4. The goal is to create momentum, and this will ease the struggle of forward progress over time.

CHAPTER 10

Focus On The Road Ahead

You're never lost as long as you have gas.

Ihope by now we can agree you are in the driver's seat of your life. If you are not in the driver's seat, we need to start the process of getting you there. Once you can embrace your role as the person in charge of your destiny, the next step is for you to decide where you want to go. Where in your love life, your finances, your career, your business, or your family do you want to go? Without a clear destination, we can't create the roadmap to get you there.

200 MILLION ROADS

A company created a map of the United States using only existing roads and streets. What they determined is that there are more than 240 million road segments in the United States. Imagine if someone called you and said simply, "Can you tell me which road I should take?" The logical response for most of us would be to ask where they were trying to go. If they had a predetermined destination, you could assist them with directions. If they did not, you would simply be naming streets with no confirmation that any of those roads would get them where they needed to be.

Life is much like this map of random roads. There are countless choices to make, endless directions you can travel, and unlimited things you can try. However, the questions you should be asking yourself constantly are, "Where am I headed? What am I trying to accomplish? Most importantly, when all is said and done, where do I want to be?" Once you determine this destination, you can then begin to identify the best way to get there.

While planning your journey, you will quickly realize there are many roads that take you to your desired destination. Some roads are paved, and some are not. Some have higher speed limits and allow you to move faster, while others roads are safer but will take you longer to get to your destination. Some are one way and others will send you in circles or down a dead end if you don't pay attention. Much like we discussed when comparing one person's reality to another person's reality, no one path is right while another path is wrong. There are a number of ways to improve your situation, accomplish your goals, and create your ideal life. It is on you to decide which path you are most comfortable taking. In order to do that, you first must be absolutely clear about where you want to go.

SIDE AND REARVIEW MIRRORS ARE FOR GLANCING

Have you ever taken time to consider how much a car is designed for how you should live your life? There are simple things in the design like whether or not you want to take one person with you (a two seater) on the journey or eight people (a van)? Do you want to play it safe in an economy vehicle or rush through in a sports car? The similarities are endless, but for the sake of this conversation, I want to focus on your ideal line of sight.

In just about every vehicle, the windshield is the largest, most important piece of glass. We are taught not to let things obstruct our view through the windshield or not let a crack in the windshield linger because it eventually will spread and impair our vision. Most importantly, the windshield is the biggest piece of glass on the car because it is designed for you to look in front of you as you move forward. It is nothing fancy or groundbreaking. Simply, keep your eyes on the road ahead of you to ensure you are always focused on where you are going. This can help you avoid any obvious issues you might be approaching.

Now, what about your side mirrors? These mirrors are placed, so you can easily use them, and they are there, so you can keep an eye on what others around you are doing. They are tiny in comparison to your windshield. Most importantly, you only truly need them if you decide to get out of your lane! Let me repeat that in bold letters. **It doesn't matter what the people next to you are doing unless you start to get out of your lane!**

So many people spend way too much time focused on their side mirrors and are concerned with what other people are doing. Those mirrors are small for a reason. They are not meant for you to spend your time staring at them. They never give you the full picture of what's happening next to you. They only show the small portion you can see during your momentary glance. Life is the same way.

We get a glance of what someone else is doing without knowing the whole picture, and we begin to focus on only that. We stare so long that we're no longer focused on our own lanes and our own destination. We lose sight of where we are going. Just as you do in a car, I believe it is safest if you occasionally glance at what is happening around you, but spend the majority of your time focused on the direction in which you're heading and try to stay in your lane.

We also can't forget about the dreaded rear view mirror. The rear view mirror is the most interesting view because it is literally stuck to your windshield. You cannot go forward and focus on the road ahead without a constant reminder of what's behind you. Much like the side mirrors, you are only supposed to glance at this mirror before putting your eyes back on the road. However, in driving, as in life, this mirror is a bit more dangerous.

Looking into a rear view mirror requires your eyes to shift focus completely. Whether you realize it or not, when you glance into your rearview mirror, your eyes have to blur the images out in the windshield, so you can focus on the smaller images in the rear view mirror. This means that although you are moving forward, when you need to look back for longer than a glance, your eyes will blur the road ahead completely. Simply put, you will lose sight of where you are going. Because of this shift in your vision, it is much more dangerous than the occasional glance in a side mirror. Life is no different.

While the occasional glance at those around you isn't beneficial, the fixation on your past has the potential to blur your vision for a better life totally and completely. This happens in every aspect of our life. We can't focus on new love because we hold onto love lost. We can't plan for tomorrow because we won't stop thinking about yesterday. We can't grab hold of a new way of thinking because we're unwilling to let go of our old way of thinking. We spend so much time in the rear view mirror, our ability to focus on the view through the windshield is compromised. You can't ignore your past just like you shouldn't ignore the cars behind you, but in life as in a car, if you don't regain a focus on the road ahead you undoubtedly will lose your direction and possibly crash on your journey.

There is a reason both the side and rear view mirrors are small in a car, and you should ensure you shrink them to their appropriate size in your life as well. They were never made for you to stare at them or fixate on them. They were made for you to glance at them. They were designed for you to assess your surroundings and increase your awareness, but they never were meant to be a distraction from the road right in front of you. Stop comparing your life and journey to those next to you when you don't have the total picture and stop looking back so often that you lose sight of where you're going.

YOU HAVE THE FUEL

When I first learned to drive, my Uncle Mikey always would tell me that as long as I had gas in my car, I would never be lost. I have to be honest and say that as a 15-year-old planning for an upcoming driving test, that made absolutely no sense to me. It wasn't until later in life that I realized what he was saying to me. Much like many things he taught me, it had much more to do with life than it had to do with the actual topic at hand.

If you are driving a car and somehow get away from your planned route, some might say you are lost. However, as long as there is gas in your car, you have the ability to continue moving until you can reorient yourself and find your way again. You may be unsure of where you are, or you may be searching for the right roads again, but you are still moving and have not given up on your journey. Therefore, you are not lost. You are simply off track a bit.

We've already discussed that the journey to your ideal life may not be easy, and it may not go exactly as planned, but that is normal. I can't tell you how many times I've gone out for a drive only to discover a detour on the only way I know how to get somewhere. It does not mean I have to go home; it simply means I have to find a new path. As long as I have fuel, I can get to my destination.

Remember, your pain is your fuel. Your past is your fuel. The life you want and the people for whom you want to create it are your fuel. If you vow not to lose sight of that, when life turns you around, and it feels like you might be on the wrong road and have lost your way, you always will have the fuel you need to keep going until you get back on the right path. A detour is not a dead end, and a dead end doesn't mean stop. Both simply mean you can't go the way you planned. Always remember, your life and purpose are the fuel you need to keep going.

TAKEAWAYS

Even without knowing the route you will take, the most important step in your journey is deciding where you want to go. What do you want from life? How do you want your life to look? What is the type of person with whom you want to share it (if you want to share it with anyone)? Once you determine those things, it is time to create a plan and start moving.

During your journey it will be key for you to remember:

1. There is no single way to reach your goal. The important thing is to pick a path and begin the journey.

2. Stay in your lane. You can look out the side mirror if you want, but you're not getting the full picture.

3. Looking back for too long causes you to lose focus on the road ahead.

4. You may get turned around or go off course, but as long as you remember why you started this journey, you will always find the fuel to keep going.

5. Don't get discouraged if you find yourself at a detour or a dead end road. There are more than 240 million roads to get you where you're going.

Epilogue

If you've made it this far, my hope is that some things have already begun to change, even if it is only the way you view the control you have over your life. You never were meant to be a passenger in your own life, and no one said it would always be pretty. Things aren't always as clear cut as we've been told they would be, but it should not stop you from reaching new levels of growth and success.

The most important thing for you to remember is that you're in the driver's seat. If you're not, you need to take back control of the steering wheel TODAY! Once you've done this, it's time to map out the road ahead. To do so, remember the 10 key points we discussed in the book:

> » Be honest about your situation. It's not good or bad. It just is.
>
> » We all have baggage, and some of it is coming for the ride so stop fighting it.
>
> » You are all you need to start. Stop waiting.
>
> » Love can be given from a distance. You may need additional space between you and those closest to you.

» The only right you should worry about is right now.

» You may feel alone, but you won't finish the journey alone. We are all connected, and those who have been where you've been want to help you get where they are.

» You may not find all the closure and forgiveness you desire. Accept it and drive on.

» Stop worrying about being right and start being better. Your reality will change as you do.

» Use your past (good or bad) to lay the foundation for your future.

» Glance around you for awareness but keep your eyes on the road ahead.

This is your life and your journey. For help on creating the roadmap to your future, please remember to visit www.imdrivingbook.com/bonus for more tools and information.

About the Author

Damian McGee is a successful business owner, renowned author, and life coach, or more accurately, a "situation coach." Driven by his compassionate personality and passion for helping other people, Damian has made it his mission to guide others on unique personal growth journeys in order to help them build better lives for themselves.

Damian's books are a blend of his life experiences intertwined with his personal struggles and a plentiful dash of his determined and inspiring version of "tough love."

Through his books, Damian shares his invaluable knowledge and strategies to overcome hardships in life - the situations and feelings that are holding people back from achieving their true potential.

He believes that people have the right to be happy and prosperous in their lives, and he wants to show them that they can achieve their full potential despite the negativity thrown their way and give them support and guidance on that journey.

Damian holds a bachelor's degree from Central Michigan University, and when he is not writing, he loves to travel and soak up diverse cultures and customs because he believes "that is the best way to enrich your life and broaden your horizons on a path to success."

Additional Resources

www.imdrivingbook.com/bonus

CPSIA information can be obtained
at www.ICGtesting.com
Printed in the USA
FSHW012033270721
83551FS

9 781736 882900